SO-APN-019

Beyond Dreams of Rescue

poems

by Mary-Ella Holst

Mary-Ella Holst

Wind Rose Press
New York, New York

Some of these poems have been published in *Conversations, Chapel Talks, Kairos, Offerings* and *Non Sequitur.*

"To Those Who Love the Night" was choreographed and first performed by Linda St. Ambrogio in New York City, in 1987.

Copyright © 1992 by Mary-Ella Holst

All rights reserved. Except for brief passages quoted in newspaper, magazine, radio or television review, no part of this book may be reproduced in any form or by any means, electronic or mechanical, including photocopying or recording, or by information storage or retrieval system, without prior written permission of the publisher.

First Edition

10 9 8 7 6 5 4 3 2

Library of Congress Cataloging in Publication Data

Holst, Mary-Ella
    Beyond Dreams of Rescue

    Poems
    I. Title
PS324.H756B [1]   1992   811'.54   92-60934

ISBN 0-9633273-0-5

Cover photograph by the author
Cover and text design by Joann Anand

Printed in the United States of America

Published by Wind Rose Press, P.O. Box 1061, Gracie Station, New York, NY 10028

To the women who were there as I moved beyond dreams of rescue:

Joann Anand, Vanessa Bell, Nancy Grey Beakel, Carol Brody, Lotus Do, Carol Friedland, Margaret Fuller, Charlotte Perkins Gilman, Joan Elias Gore, Yvonne Groseil, Brenda Lee Hall, Marianna Hill, Mary Spencer Hohl, Ruth McCullough Holst, Beate Wheeler Holst, Helen Hornburg, Marie Jenney Howe, Arlene Icart, Thelma Louise Mehling, Kinsey Millhone, Harris Riordan, Linda St. Ambrogio, Sara Silverman, Elizabeth Cady Stanton, Abigail Ford Strong, Angie Henry Utt,

and to the two women who have most shaped my life:

Patricia Hall Infante
Darcy Hall

Contents

Beyond Dreams of Rescue

Endangered Species

I. 1941

When I was a child, during the war –
1941 or '42 –
I dreamed I was a captive in a dark
and foreign city
where each night I escaped the orphanage
that was my prison
and ran, recurringly, through the back alleys
of blacked-out streets.

On the porch of the orphanage was a great swan,
a wooden contraption,
for the amusement of the children
and each night as I ran, ran until my body
would burst,
an unseen hand pressed a button
and slowly the swan would extend,
elongate its great body
until its neck curved around my waist.
Then
it retracted its creaking body until
I dangled there, over the porch
of the orphanage in the dark and foreign city.

And yet, I cannot say, even now, what
would have become of me had the swan
not captured me.

II. 1986

On an English summer afternoon of
    Queen Anne's lace,
shelducks, coots and ruddy-headed geese,
in the earnest theme park of the waterfowl
    sanctuary
we adopt a Bewick swan.

In the December dusk of the Severn estuary
the great birds crash out of the sky
and shatter the crust of wetland ice.
The Bewick swan has returned.
Now for the English winter there is the capture,
the count, the reading of the bands.
Bewick swans mate for life
but ours, named Otoo, travels alone.

At dawn on a February morning the great birds
will rise from the misted waters and not return
... until next year.
They will pass over Chernobyl
and coast the wind drafts as they travel north.

Otoo will not return.
She is lost. She has been dropped from the list.

The Lottery

I. The Lottery

Two hundred million sperm lunged forward.
I won.

II. Sleeping with Cops

Sometimes
when I feel desperate and frail
I want to sleep with a cop.
I want to feel terribly small.
Sometimes I need to feel
neat and obsessive and clean.

Freedom is painful.

Sometimes I sink to the floor
on my knees
in the midst of the half-read books,
the unfinished letters
and I want to die
or live in a cradle.
I want an ultimate father, assurances,
and lies.

III. Democracy

Democracy is my mother.
From this matrix I emerge
into shadows, into shapes
that I make real.

IV. The Prize

What is this raging prize I've won?
Amid the agony and confrontation,
the endless compromises and complete surprises
I sometimes think I know.

Darkness befriends me, something stirs.
Someone responds. It is I.
I, alone and complete,
for an instant before the fragments
shudder and realign
in imperfect harmony.

Sometimes my body seems to recall
the loneliness and ecstasy of meteors.

Credo

Death is the great and gaping wound
that splatters
through the life of the living.

When I was a child,
my teacher
taught me how to pull a paint-drenched
    toothbrush
across a piece of window screen.
The paint would fly in all directions
except where the designs we had cut
were layered on the paper.
Then after rinsing my hands
I would lift the layers
and where the designs had lain
all was pure, pristine, untouched by paint.

It was a lie.

There is no pure, unsplattered space.
Purity is an illusion, a human abstraction.
The layers of our own design will not
protect us.

The great and gaping wound
sprays its vulnerability into hidden crevices
and festers there.
There are a thousand traces, caught,
    commingled
and all needing the rinsing waters.

Go to the well, run to the beach
and rest in the waters floating.
Float and scrub, float and scrub
and be sad when it is over.

It is not over.
We have splattered our lives
across a Universe.

We cannot hide under the layers
of our own design.
We can, of course, turn away,
turn just so, at such an angle
that we learn that we cannot raise
our eyes or turn our heads –
and frozen, rigid in time, we pose
as statues with no eyes.

To move, to see, we must look,
and recognize the wound as our own birth.

Face to face with our own death,
only one word is spoken:

Life.

Life eases, life heals, life affirms
    itself;
Life, passionate, arbitrary, fragile.

Life informed by its own astonished survival
is the balm of the great and gaping wound.

Yes

Lost in the labyrinth
confronted by a no
at every turn
tortured by nits and not
wearied by hypocritical beckonings
it is startling to hear
a sigh of yes.

the yes that crumbles walls
and reveals the sunlight slightly
through the brambles
that remain upright and tough and tearing.

we must find our own way
but the balm of yes
yes – life   life – yes
lets us live along the path, bleeding vibrant blood.

the sensual yes
the yes of silence
the sensory yes
the mystical yes
merge until
yes   yes   yes

yes
yes evil exists but I am not evil
yes good exists but I am not good
I am and I choose.

More than a paradox of perspective:
the brambles remain
and I am free.

yes – life   yes   life – yes
yes and free.

I See Death in the Distance

I see death in the distance,
not a mirage,
not a shimmering oasis
but a reality
glimpsed,
one more responsibility.

I see death through the dense distractions
of the present,
not a shadow,
not an illusion of air and light
but inevitability,
known now.

I see death on the horizon
rising as a ship's sails rise.
The ship sails for me
but it is not the ship I love,
it is the sea.

Child of the Holocaust

I.

The knock upon the door
at midnight
and the leaving.

Riding on a train
through strange languages
the sound of shots
the familiar language
is silent.

Channel crossing.
Separation.
Ocean crossing.
Abyss.

Somehow we all survived
and our scars are buried
with the bodies
of our friends.

II.

Mystery shrouds
the raw edge of nerves,
the paralyzing terror,
the robot response,
the right answers,
the importance of being a
pretty child,
the unreported incidents of deceit.
It happened.
Nothing more.

III.

> The trains do not run
> anymore.
> The timetable is lost
> packed away in the
> baggage.
> If we lose the train
> do we lose the tracks?

IV.

> Today's child
> is born from that abyss
> from the denied womb
> of the silent language
> haunted by shots
> unheard.
> Child to child,
> they speak in foreign tongues,
> each to each.

V.

Reality lies
in that abyss,
the ocean of the world
from which we all, everychild, emerge
scarred.
Terrorized by loss,
stunned by separation,
fighting for control of self
and world,
whirlpools, undercurrents, until, finally,
we are washed ashore.

VI.

And, then, we must do it again.
Every time. Every child. Every love.
Every leaving.
Every awareness of self.
Each birth. Each death.
Each one. One by one.

Sanctuary

Sanctuary is an attitude
of solitude.

Protection is an act
of love.

Daring out upon the slippery
rock
I cut my cheek and
cried.

And as I wiped my hand
across
my bloody face I tasted
tears.

Alone
I could have wept
forever
perhaps lamenting a scar.

Strange
how I tripped on a rock
that I now carry in my
pocket.

The Bog

At the frayed edges of my soul
the grasses begin to grow
weaving new green mats
to catch the delicate roots
of a new day, morning sun.

When the grass mat forms a bed,
first, the flower, then, the fruit
mature to seed; then, the step.
Still the dampness seeps through
wherever I am.
There is danger in the bog.

To fall through, now, deep into the unconscious,
darkness without oxygen,
would halt forever the decay that is the growth.
Each footprint catches but a cup.

Hidden, now, the lake that was;
the bog is formed.
Underground, the water runs clear.
On the surface, small flowers bloom.

Alexandra at Coffee Hour
or
The Kingdom of the Survivor

Alexandra.
Born. Diagnosed. Expected to die.
The heart too weak; the body too frail,
    tiny, traumatized.

"The doctors," they say, "performed a miracle."
"Our prayers," they say, "were answered."

Alexandra,
namesake of a conqueror and a queen,
summons her regal heritage in a sneer
and marches in total command
toward the coffee cake.

She cuts a swath, unerringly
dividing the assembled precisely in half.
Half will credit science.
Half will credit God.

But there is one vote uncounted.
Who has asked Alexandra?

The decisive voter seems unconcerned,
eating coffee cake, flirting with her father,
chasing her bunny muff across the floor.

Alexandra!
Stop muffing around and vote!

Alexandra,
namesake of a conqueror and a queen
is bored, wishes to leave, and will.
Her father lifts her above the intellectual,
    theological, coffee-cup roar.

        images . . .
            of tubes and transfusions, incisions,
            intensive confusions and the sputtering,
            struggling, triumphant will to survive . . .
        float in her path.

Who claims victory?

Alexandra does.
And in her exit sweep
not once will she look back
upon those who can not or will not
vote for themselves.

Odysseus

Odysseus sailed into the sun
blazing through dazzling
patterns
of sunrise, sunset
while the poet judged
life
by the breeze.

Burned and brutalized
by sea and sun
by myth of manhood
in search of what we are taught
we ought to be,
Odysseus lives.
Immortality is strung upon a lyre.

Understanding darkness,
the poet
will not be blinded to life
by death.

Seduced by words of glory,
by images of gods,
we are trapped for an eternal moment
in the poet's web
(woven of sensuous mist and subtle shade).
Caught, now we must glimpse,
although we may yet only half remember
the blinding truth
of this world.

Softly, in the breeze that blows
small boats of bark and leaf,
our conscious dreams are carried
toward the unconscious sea
where raging storms have yet
to sink
the small rafts of life
we craft of words and deeds.

Come, he says, look at life,
understand your journey,
find beauty, soar inward,
see.

Generation

For Harris, on Her Thirtieth Birthday

I. Thirty Years Ago (1954)

> Twenty is the age to be a poet
> (not to write, but to be a poet)
> or to wander in a labyrinth of words
> without a string.
> To cut strings and weave small pieces
> bound, if at all, by smiles
> and tears.
> Twenty is a time for forgetting
> memories,
> a time for unbinding.

II. Twenty Years Ago (1964)

> Thirty is the age of patterns,
> a time of recognition
> that all these strings collect
> and tangle
> and are torn
> and there is mending to be done.
> And a pattern emerges:
> depth and dimension
> and, most strangely, discipline.
> We know how to sew.

III. Today (1984)

Half a century later
I am a person composed of poems
and memories
quilting and connecting on a thread
of friends and love
patterns and pieces that cannot be undone.

We are always weaving,
collecting strings, mending and sewing,
knotting and not counting.
Only knowing that we sew.

Menses

Ancient measuring moon,
Waxing, pregnant;
Full, birthing stars;
Waning into mystery!

Caught in the web of your rhythm,
I travel the Universe in your wet wake.
The tides are full in me
and I move to ancient images of water
mixed with blood and salt.
Your oceans move in me
mixing my own blood with possibility.
Possibility and time, waxing, waning.
Salt tracks on waterless sands
trace the web that cradles me,
cradles, catches, holds and binds me
to ancient rhythms, rocking yet.

Eleven Generations

Eleven generations ago my times-eight-great
grandfather arrived in this country.
Of his thirteen children, three survived.
It seems if one could survive childbirth, child-bearing,
occasional plagues, persistent hunger,
six-hour sermons and one's own self-righteousness,
Death came quietly.

My generation narrowly missed being born
    in speakeasies,
taxicabs and other socially inconvenient places.
All survived.
We die with more drama.
For one, death came while lighting a match.
He was dead while the match still burned.

Our children, delivered and attended, arrive
unbreeched, on time, with flowers.
What have we taught our children about death?

Death came quietly to my times-eight-great grandfather
in 1699 at the age of 94.
What had he learned about life from his ten dead
children?

Our Children Are Wondrous Images

Our children are wondrous images
who reflect us
as we forgot we were and, as they see, we
still are.

The children act out our unconscious fantasies
and the young sing the dreams
we gave away.

It is hard to love our own lost courage.

The young have an unerring sense
of who will and who won't
and the days when we can
and the days when we cannot.

Today, if I can be who I am
without apology,
what dazzling courage
the young will see,
what possibility there is for love.

Meditation While Chopping Celery

Slice. Slice. Slice. Turn the stalk and chop. Sometimes I
count . . . twenty-three, twenty-four, twenty-five . . . and
then lose myself in the light green miracle of water
clinging to the strings of fiber. I chop well. Forty years
of chopping celery, slicing zucchini, shaving onions. I
work quickly and surely. I have mastered the knife. Oh!
the colors I have seen, the textures I have felt at my
fingertips, the crackles I have heard in forty years of
chopping celery.

In the beginning I was a mere apprentice: washing,
watching. My apprenticeship was over when I married.
Chop, chop, slice, measure, more. And divorce. Chop,
chop, slice, slice. And death, measure, more. Cutting.
And my children. Carrots, celery, peppers, cucumbers,
broccoli, cabbage. And bread.

Today it is two quarts of celery, a part of sixty portions of
pasta for the hungry people who are homeless. Wash,
rinse, slice, turn the stalk and chop. Now that it is
effortless, age is beginning to gnarl my hands. I am
master of the knife, mistress of the board. Sure, complete
for this two-quart time. Feeding others, feeding myself.
At home because I am lost in chopping celery.

Love Poems

There Is a Rhythm to Innocence

There is a rhythm to innocence
and experience, to knowing and not knowing,
An ancient rhythm glimpsed in seasons,
echoed at the ocean's shore,
An ancient rhythm that cannot be tuned
nor honed nor locked nor caught nor caged.

Innocence expects or demands precision,
design and control. Or drama.
Experience is wholly human and welcomes
a night's rest, a routine day, and retains
a strange confidence in kindness.

There is a rhythm to relationship,
An ancient rhythm of innocence and knowing,
of change and unchanging.

Ocean and sand and ever-changing edge,
racing sand, unceasing waters,
Somewhere there must be a piece of seaweed
to mark, to measure. A rock. A shell.
Anything to say, "Here. Here we are."

This much we know:
There is no way to measure love.
Nor our beginning. Nor the end.

A mystery, an ancient one:
How is it that I love?
I do not know how to love.
But do.

It is an answer, my loving you,
    to a question I could not form,
A resolution, an understanding
    of a dream I cannot remember.
It is a dance I cannot dance alone.

It is a rhythm, an ancient rhythm,
    not heard, not felt, not seen
But known in the experience of you.

Chaos

Chaos –
And in the dark, a star.
Steadfast,
and a tangle of ropes at the mooring.

Time melts, stretches.
Distance is compacted, shatters.
These journeys are treacherous
not because of great waves
but by becalming.

Traveler, return.
No answer.
Traveler, come home.
No answer.
Only movement.

Silent undercurrents shiver.
Words fall like rain on forgotten days.
There is movement, a shift, a strain.
A rope unties itself by chance
or by design.

These journeys defy gravity.
Meaning moves upside-down in dreams
and night moves into day
lit only by a star.

Traveler, turn back.
No answer.
Traveler, traveler.
No answer.
Only movement.

There is a crackling in the air.
The rain will come.
There is movement, a drift, and direction.

And love explodes through the universe
of you.

A Single Leaf Shimmers

A single leaf shimmers
in the moonlight
as in autumn flight
it pauses to play with the wind.

The wind wanders through
the evening
seeking diversion from
its eternal becoming.

What is play but touching?
But meeting? Here.
Here on an autumn afternoon.
Remembering and waiting for the moon.

Marriage

"I love you because you will not marry anyone but me."
– from a Vietnamese love song

Truth is not words
    but being.

The words are ambiguous:
    I want you here. Now.
The words play games:
    I want you here. Now.

We are not children but our
    childhoods are not lost.
Nor are the nations, the cultures,
    the quietude, the defiance,
    that brought us here, today.

We have chosen to speak
    not in language but in music
    and art and being.
We have chosen to marry.

Marriage says only:
    Truth.

[For Lotus Do and Christopher Brooks, 1987]

The Dance

Spiral

[To accompany movement by children]

Growing, spiraling, growing.
Spiral.

Circling, circling, circling
wider.

Twirling, whirling, swirling.
Grow.

Slowly, surely, snail-like
growing.

Spiraling, growing, spiraling.
Grow.

To Those Who Love the Night

I. Invocation

> Oh, Heresy! Oh, Dream!
> My quest begins in Thee.
> Mother, forget not Thy child,
> Nightly, I return to Thee.

II. Ode to the Night

> Fragile light of moon and leaf shadow,
> Wind-tossed, gentle errant.
> Silence, born of sleeping birds,
> Pierced, now and then, pierced.
> Ancient smokeless fires flare
> And die before the day.
> And stones.
> The stones are set to mark the dawn.
> Night, O truly blessed night, sister
> To our dreams, brother of desire,
> Lead the way.

III. The Trial of Mary Esty

> Mary Esty, ancient martyr, Mary Esty,
> Bedeviled by the day.
>
> Wife and woman, Mary, mother, stand!
> Stand accused!
> Accursed woman, hast thou knowledge?
> Sower of herbs, what secret dost thou keep?
> Healer, what magic thou command?
> Ancient mother, hang and be damned!
> Thy beloved serpent turns to rope!
> Thy ancient gods become gallow tree!

Hang! Mary Esty, hang!
Vile Eve, evil woman, death to thee!

IV. Lament for Mary Esty

Mary, mother, good woman, good wife,
Daughter of adventure, midwife to a continent,
Swing, thou, gently in the raging winds of day.
Freedom grieves the spirit that gives it birth.
Thy labors are fulfilled.
The night renews the quest.
Rest, now, gentle, spirit-mother, rest.

V. The Conception of Freedom

The restless, wakeful dreamers of the dream
Echo through the night in whistles,
Cries and callings to a yonder shore.
Oh! America!
Freedom's dream in daylight!
Thy soul was dreamed in darkness,
Visioned into being on the ancient plain,
By the light of fires that smoulder in the souls
Of the tyrant's child.

VI. Homecoming

Rise now, gentle-devouring moon,
Welcome home thy children,
Singers of night's song,
Dancers of the dream.

*[Mary Esty was hanged on September 22, 1692,
on Gallows Hill, Salem, Massachusetts.]*

49

Song: A Libretto for the Dance

The characters of the play:
Young Woman
Young Man
Old Woman
Old Man

PROLOGUE
When the stage is lighted, all four are seen:

Young Woman:
Bring me a fire that is green.
Light it with your eyes and
tender it with
kisses.

Young Man:
Swing me from an orange tree
that I may shake the blossoms
to the ground
one by
one.

Old Woman:
Where has that bastard gone?
They say he died but I
lived sixty years
to know they
lied.

Old Man:
How many times can you eat
an apple?
How many times have you
tried?

Old Man:
    Apple

Young Man:
    Orange

Young Woman:
    Fire

Old Woman:
    Died

Young Woman:
    Kisses

Old Woman:
    Lied

Old Man:
    How many?

Young Man:
    One by one.

THE WAY OF THE DREAM

Young Woman:
    I dreamed I saw him on
    a small black horse
    and I am ashamed because
    a horse should be white.

But he came, but he came
and for one brief hour
there was a small green
flame.

Young Man:
Little Blossom, I come to pluck you.
I come to smell the perfume of your
hair.

I come to wait upon you,
to linger over you a
moment.

Young Woman:
And do you think I am to be
caught
in your web of preposterous
delight?

Young Man:
Come, let me catch you.
Jump. . . . Leap. . . . Do not be
afraid.

Young Woman:
There is a certain joy. . .

Young Man:
You are right. There is.

Young Woman:
Hush, if we are too eager
it will be over.

And let us think of it
while we wait
for ourselves.

Young Man:
Think? Never!
Act. Always!

Hop to the scotch
and swing tomorrow
through forever.
Jump
    and stop midair to
contemplate the joy of coming down
again.
    That is long enough to wait.

Young Woman:
I could wait . . .

Young Man:
Never!

Young Woman:
And when it is over
I shall dream of this moment
forever.

Young Man:
I hardly think so.

Young Woman:
You never think but
I hope you do
enjoy.

Young Man:
How long must this
game continue?
Time is not waiting for
grace.

Young Woman:
It ought to.

Young Man:
Someday for you it may.
But tonight
it is I
who will not wait.

Young Woman:
Oh why must I, why
succumb to such pleasure
when resistance makes it
stay?

Young Man:
You succumb to pleasure
simply for
pleasure.

Young Woman:
You are right,
my knight, my ever-after
dream.
I succumb.
And the flame,
where is the flame?

Young Man:
    I will light it now.
    I will call upon the mist
    and I will beckon to the rain.
    And the snow will come
    and the sun will shine
    and tonight,
    tonight, you are
    mine.

Young Woman:
    I want to run upon the
    sand until my feet are
    smoothed to ivory and when
    I fall,
    let it be in your lap.

    I want to ever smell the pine
    and ever touch the scar.

    Say sweet things to me
    and let me believe the
    nonsense
    of this moment.

    The sweet and utter
    nonsense
    will be my forever
    treasure.

Young Man:
    Your nonsense is your
    own.
       And it makes you beautiful.

Young Woman:
Will you take me to a place
that I have never
known
and sweep me from the world?

Young Man:
A soft brown darkness
will encircle you
and tell you not
to fear.

You will be safe.

Young Woman:
I know, I know.
Do not reassure me
or the danger will
reappear.

Young Man:
Tell me what you know.

Young Woman:
A soft gray cloud
floats against an azure sky
and succumbs to the darkness.
This is night.
Night tells me to dream

And I dream
too well.

*The stage is darkened and as the lights are raised again,
the Old Man and the Old Woman are sitting
wrapped in a huge old quilt. They are giggling:*

Old Man:
> I had bitten of the apple
> and had chewed upon the core.
> I had spit a seed or two
> and thought I'd eat no more.

Old Woman:
> Ah . . .

Old Man:
> Who would believe it?

Old Woman:
> My son would choke upon his
> beer.
> Oh, dear, dear, dear.

Old Man:
> They wouldn't believe it.

Old Woman:
> They wouldn't believe it.

Old Man:
> Then let's not tell them.

They fall backwards under the quilt giggling as the lights are dimmed. When the lights are raised, the Young Woman is eating an orange and the Old Man is polishing an apple. The Old Woman is folding the quilt as the Young Man prepares to go away:

Young Man:
> What have you there,
> old woman?

Old Woman:
  Get on your way, young man
  I don't need youth
  anymore.

Young Man:
  You must be very old –
  older than the morning,
  older than the spring.
  You must be very old.

Old Woman:
  I am one day older than
  you.
  One tomorrow.
  It takes but one yesterday
  to have been
  young.
  And one tomorrow
  to be old.

Young Man:
  I do not believe you.
  Isn't there a willow limb
  that I could bend?

Old Woman:
  To bend me you would
  need an ax.
  Branches are for bending
  but old stumps like me
  are a waste of time.

I can give you nothing but
life.
And that you will take for yourself.

Young Man:
It is not a life I need.
I have a life
and rather like it too.
But I wonder, old woman,
is there something else
I can take from you?

Old Woman:
Nothing.
An old quilt?
Here, take it.

Young Man:
A blanket?
Moth-eaten, unkempt
and wet with rot
of decaying men
who died yesterday
or the day before?
An old blanket
to shelter me from what?
A wind that will not blow
tonight?
A cold that has yet to sleep
with me?

Forget your blanket, old woman,
it is useless
but for covering a dying
heart
or a broken body.

Old Woman:
I am folding up this blanket now.
I offer it to you.
Leave it here, come back for it
tomorrow
when you will need it.

Young Man:
Here, take your blanket.
It befits you.
It is yours.
It will keep you warm when
tonight you sleep alone.

Old Woman:
And there is a certain
peace in that.

Young Man:
Then, madam, I choose war
and will bravely face it.

He starts to leave, then turns and says:

And shall we meet upon this road
some bright sad tomorrow?

Old Woman:
Never on this road, sir.

The dust upon our tracks has
met and is mingled underneath
us now.
It will rain
and a bud will open
and fall
and grow
in the mud of our feet.

Young Man:
Perhaps it will blossom.

Old Woman:
And perhaps it will die.

She is alone.

Perhaps, perhaps
tomorrow or another day.
Who knows?
Not I.

She covers herself with the quilt.

Nor do I care to know.

*The Old Man returns; he is eating –
an apple, of course.*

Old Man:
When I was younger
and somewhat wiser
I would gaze upon
my knuckle
and think
it will be with me
until I die.
And here it is.

The same knuckle
grown a little stiff
perhaps but still willing
to bend.

But what has happened to my hair?
What stays and
what goes away?

*The Young Woman enters; she is
peeling her orange. The Old Man watches her:*

To hell with apples!

He follows her.

Young Woman:
Old man, why do you follow
me?

Old Man:
It is the scent of a forgotten
fruit.

Young Woman:
Go away, take my orange
if you desire
but follow me no more.

Old Man:
Go away?
I have been away
and I will yet go
further.
Do not be afraid.

It is not my intent
to harm.

Young Woman:
I am waiting for my lover.
He will return
tonight
to see me
not you.

Old Man:
Who can say what your
lover will find
when he does choose
to stop this way
once more.

Young Woman:
You are mad.

Old Man:
Not yet.
Any day that awaits
but there must be
one clear hour
left yet in me.

I have dreamed of
madness. Known purple
locusts to chew about my ears
and silver rats to glide about my
    bed.
I have seen a smokeless fire
more than one time this year.

The thunder has signaled to me
and I have taken up its cry.
But tonight I am not mad.
I know what I am about.

Young Woman:
No.

Old Man:
I summon to my bones
strength I had forgotten.
I summon to my eyes
a scene I thought forever
passed.

Young Woman:
How can you hold me so?
I should be able to beat
upon you, break away and kill.
But I cannot.
But I will.
I will kill you
with my heart.
And in my silent thoughts I shall
murder you every moment of my
life.

And if I die tonight
and if you hang tomorrow
the battle will not be over,
old and cruel and disgusting man.

Old Man:
> You think me crude and vulgar
> but I cannot wait to argue
> to dissipate the glory
> of my hanging.
>
> An unnatural time is a time
> to die. Die by yourself
> and you admit death.
> Let someone kill you and you die young.
>
> But I shall not die,
> nor shall you.
> What shall pass tonight
> will bring me a mad and shaking
> pleasure
> and for you only a short
> discomfort.
> It will not be the last time
> you are put to pain
> for pleasure.
> You are young and do not know
> we can forget this tomorrow.

Young Woman:
> Oh help me!
> I cannot forget.
> What kind of beast, what kind
> of man
> are you?
>
> Oh help me! I am failing
> in my fight.

Old Man:
>
> Oh help me to continue to
> the end of mine.
> I bring you no ill of intent.
> What will be tonight will be but
> a variance of your pleasure.

Young Woman:
>
> You are wrong.
> Your thunder and your fire
> will be in every small flame of
> my life.

Old Man:
>
> I enrich you.

Young Woman:
>
> Oh give me the power to hate.
> Oh give me the strength to despise.
> What I hear tonight are a madman's
>   lies.

Old Man:
>
> Only a lover lies.

Young Woman:
>
> Upon whom can I call in
> my lonely prayer?
> Where is there a soul
> that can hear a silent
> scream?
>
> You are mad.
> Tell me you are mad.
> It will make it easier to bear.

Old Man:
>I am not mad.
>I am not evil.
>I am human.
>Isn't that enough
>to explain my madness?

Young Woman:
>I fear the fire of hell.
>I dream the dream of salvation.

Old Man:
>Enough of heaven and hell.
>We are here tonight
>and tonight the earth awaits me
>and you.

Young Woman:
>I am dead.

Old Man:
>You are alive.
>That is your charm.

He throws her down upon the blanket and the lights are darkened. When the lights are raised, she is on the blanket; the Old Man is gone. As she speaks, the Old Woman stirs:

Young Woman:
>Help me. I do not know
>what is happening.

Old Woman:

> My child, what are you
> doing here?
> What has happened to you?

Young Woman:

> My flesh has been torn
> by a toothless jaw.

Old Woman:

> What foul lover has ripped
> you thus?

> Hush, do not speak.
> I will comfort you
> and make you
> whole again.
> My God, the blood has seeped
> beneath the blanket to
> the ground.

Young Woman:

> Hold my hand.
> I do not want to die
> without my mother.

Old Woman:

> I hold your hand.
> I am your mother.

> And I am grieved by this
> death.

The Young Man enters.

Young Man:
>Hail, good woman,
>the road is yet
>the same.
>We meet again.

Old Woman:
>The road is not the same.
>It is yet another
>color.

Young Man:
>What hide you in your blanket?
>What lies covered there?
>A sweet surprise for you?

Old Woman:
>It is no surprise.
>It is but another sad
>discovery.

Young Man:
>I bend myself to uncover
>your secret.

The Young Man lifts the cover.

>Can I ever stand again?
>Why is she dead?
>Why did she die?

When I saw her last she did
lie
but not with this look upon her
face.

Old Woman:
Do you know this woman?

Young Man:
I knew her for one brief time.
And yet I did think I
made her happy.
I did think.
I did.

I will avenge this death
of the happiness I created.
I will search this place
and I will kill the beast
and quarter him asunder.

Old Woman:
Go search if you must.
Look about this place
and recognize him if you can.

He leaves.

Old Woman:
And now, my child,
I will comfort thee.
I will take you as carefully
as it is possible to carry

a broken heart
and cover you with dust
while your lover searches the wind
to repay this lust.

She leaves the blanket and drags the body to be buried.
The lights dim and when they are raised, the Old Man is
upon the blanket.

Old Man:
    Woman, where are you?
    I want you just the way you were
    before I set upon my adventure.
    I am afraid.
    I am afraid of that gay creature
    whom I do not understand.
    She will haunt me forever.
    Where has she gone?

Old Woman:
    What now is upon my blanket
    to bury?

Old Man:
    Old woman, you are changed.
    What has happened to
    you?

Old Woman:
    What has happened?
    I have buried love.
    I have tried to keep it
    and it has slipped away.

This time it was a young woman
who knew one brief hour of joy
and died in perfect memory of that.
Another it was a babe unborn,
another it was . . .
But why recount?
Why remember?
Blot out the ways in
which I grow old.

Old Man:
  Are you mad?

Old Woman:
  Just old.
  And fearful of the burying
  I have yet to do.

Old Man:
  Do not talk of fear.
  I am afraid
  and I do not like to hear it
  mentioned.

Old Woman:
  I see blood upon your hands.
  Did you murder that young girl?

Old Man:
  Do not speak of murder.

Old Woman:
  Lie down and go to sleep.

I understand you and
I will protect you because
I can do no other.
I am no longer young but
just an irrational old mother.
Sleep. Sleep and dream your dreams
of the world the way you wish it.

A sad task of protection awaits
me now.
I will find a weapon to protect
you from the reality of life.
And I will introduce
death once more in this place.

She kills him.

And once more I cover
up and bury in the ground
and in the dirt
and in among the decaying leaves
and in among my heart
an action of humanity.

Sleep. Sleep. Sleep.
And find an unearthly peace.

The Young Man returns.

Young Man:
Old woman, I saw a sign of struggle
but I do not know
with whom my battle will be fought.

Old Woman:
>Nor do I.
>What battle is before you
>I cannot see.
>But this fight, this victory
>belong to me.

>>And I have lost.

Young Man:
>>I do not understand.
>>I do not understand you
>>or what has happened here tonight.
>>I am here to watch.
>>But I do not understand.

Old Woman:
>>I have avenged the death.
>>You do not understand.
>>The murderer will soon lie
>>buried.

>>Go now. Erase forever all but
>>one thought of this place and time.
>>You brought a love
>>you do not understand.
>>The rest belongs to someone else.

>>And will you take the blanket
>>now?
>>>Carry it away with you.
>>It will warm you if you grow old.
>>It has no beauty now.
>>But wait, wait until
>>tomorrow.

Young Man:
    I feel apart.
    I do not understand.
    It has gone beyond the
    simple pleasure I did seek.

Old Woman:
    Explanations only add to
    confusion.
    Do not clutter the thought
    of a gift
    with logic.

    Let your one act of being
    float forever on a cloud
    just out of reach.
    If you try to touch it,
    it cannot be there.
    But I ramble on. I ramble on.
    It is a great fault of mine.

Young Man:
    I take this talisman
    though for what reason
    I know not.

Old Woman:
    Leave me alone.
    Go now and go back to where
    you were.

He takes the blanket.

Let the dust upon it
remind you of this road.
Look upon it with its stains
of twigs and bark
and know that you were loved.
That will serve you well one day.

He kisses her lightly on the cheek and she him.

Young Man :
I feel that I have kissed you
once before.

Old Woman:
Go. Go with sweet remembrance
and sad forgetfulness.

He leaves.

Old Woman:
I sit now to die.
But I cannot.
I try to evoke a smoke
that cannot burn for me.
What has happened here
is just my life.

Was I blind for a moment to
the identity of my own soul?

I was that girl.
That lover once was mine.

And now I sit alone
as ever lonely
as ever wanting to be loved.
The night is gone.
What now awaits me?

What tortures will a human heart invent
to inflict upon itself?
And the Old Man?
What of the Old Man?
What of him except I want him
back again.

For the Carolyn Dorfman
Dance Company

Scrabble, dog and dash.
Drip dry.
Oh, Muse of the Dance:
Why?

To move. To move with pleasure
    and precision.
To jump. To jump with ease
    and momentum.
To romp. To romp in costumes
    the color of daffodils.
To fly. To fly? No. Dancers do not fly.
Muses do.

       Balanchine's preference for bone
       doomed
       several generations of young women and
       men until
            one
               or
                   two
          began
             to
               say

     I will dance the dance.
       It will not dance me.

Oh, Muse of the Dance:
Sit in the audience tonight, bring roses,
clap, cry.

Muse, I do not know why I dance.
I dance to circumnavigate and celebrate.
I dance to damn, to deny and dream.
I dance to remember and to resolve.
Muse, I dance to move with pleasure
    and go round again.
Muse, I dance for fun. I dance for power.

Muse. Muse? Muse!
Why are you smiling?

About the Author

Mary-Ella Holst was born in Detroit and grew up in the Midwest. She is a graduate of the University of Toledo and holds a Master's degree in counseling from New York University. She has worked as a vocational guidance counselor, and is Director of Religious Education Emerita at The Unitarian Church of All Souls in New York City.

Holst's other works include *Fire Island*, a poetic drama about Margaret Fuller and Julia Ward Howe, written in the manner of the Japanese Noh theatre. She has lectured and published a number of articles on women's history, including a study of the friendship and political collaboration between Elizabeth Cady Stanton and Susan B. Anthony.

Holst, who lives in Manhattan with her husband, Guy C. Quinlan, is a volunteer tutor and fund-raiser at the Booker T. Washington Learning Center in East Harlem. She also serves on the board of the Unitarian Universalist Service Committee, an international human rights agency. She has two adult daughters and three grandchildren.

 Produced at The Print Center., Inc., 225 Varick St., New York, NY 10014, a non-profit facility for literary and arts-related publications. (212) 206-8465